LIVEWIRE INVESTIGATES

The FA Cup

Andy Croft

Oxfordshire County Council
Woodeaton Manor School
Woodeaton
Oxford
OX3 9TS
(01865) 558722

Published in association with The Basic Skills Agency

Hodder & Stoughton
A MEMBER OF THE HODDER HEADLINE GROUP

Copyright photographs:

Internal: p. 3 © Ben Radford/Allsport; p. 6 © Empics; pp. 11, 21, 26 © PA Photos; p. 14 © Allsport/Hulton/Archive; p. 18 © Allsport Hulton Deutsch/ALLSPORT
Cover: PA Photos

Orders: please contact Bookpoint Ltd, 130 Milton Park, Abingdon, Oxon OX14 4SB. Telephone: (44) 01235 827720. Fax: (44) 01235 400454. Lines are open from 9.00–6.00, Monday to Saturday, with a 24 hour message answering service. You can also order through our website www.hodderheadline.co.uk.

British Library Cataloguing in Publication Data
A catalogue record for this title is available from the British Library

ISBN 0 340 87147 4

First Published   2003
Impression number 10 9 8 7 6 5 4 3 2 1
Year   2007 2006 2005 2004 2003

Copyright © Andy Croft 2003

All rights reserved. No part of this publication may be reproduced or transmitted in any form or by any means, electronic or mechanical, including photocopy, recording, or any information storage and retrieval system, without permission in writing from the publisher or under licence from the Copyright Licensing Agency Limited. Further details of such licences (for reprographic reproduction) may be obtained from the Copyright Licensing Agency Limited, of 90 Tottenham Court Road, London W1T 4LP.

Cover photo from
Typeset by Fakenham Photosetting Limited, Fakenham, Norfolk
Printed in Great Britain for Hodder & Stoughton Educational, a division of Hodder Headline, 338 Euston Road, London NW1 3BH by Bath Press Ltd., Bath.

Contents

		Page
1	The People's Game	1
2	Beginnings	4
3	Cup Fever	7
4	Giant-killers	9
5	The White Horse Final	13
6	The Matthews Final	16
7	Did You Know?	19
8	Some FA Cup Stats	23
9	We're Going to Wembley	27

1 The People's Game

The FA Challenge Cup
is the oldest football competition
in the world.
It is the most famous football competition
in the world.

Every club in England and Wales can enter.
Every club has a chance to reach the final.
It doesn't matter if your club
is rich and famous or small and unknown.
All the names go into the draw.
Who is your club going to play
in the next round?
Who would you choose?

Big clubs and small clubs.
Big fish and tiny minnows.
Football giants and football giant-killers.
Professionals and amateurs.
Thrills and spills.
Excitement and heart-break.
Cheers and tears.
Heroes and villains.

Every season there are
hundreds of FA Cup games,
and thousands of goals.
But only one winner.

There are lots of football competitions
all over the world.
But there is only one FA Cup.

The FA Cup.

2 Beginnings

The FA Cup began in 1871.
Football was a new game then.
The rules were still changing.
Not many people played football.

The FA decided to hold a competition.
It was called the FA Challenge Cup.
They bought a cup for £20.

There were not many football clubs
in those days.
They were all amateurs.
Only fifteen clubs entered the first FA Cup.
They were mostly from London.
The Scottish team, Queens Park, entered.
They were the best team in Scotland.
The first FA Cup games were played on
11 November 1871.
Three teams didn't turn up.
The Civil Service team only had eight players.
When Crystal Palace drew with Hitchen,
both teams were allowed through to the next round.
Because Queens Park had so far to travel,
they were allowed through to the semi-final.
They drew with Wanderers
but they couldn't afford to come back to London
for the replay.
So Wanderers went through to the final.

The first FA Cup final was played
on 16 March 1872 at the Oval,
the home of Surrey cricket club.
A crowd of over 2,000 people
saw the Wanderers beat Royal Engineers 1–0.
The first FA Cup final goal
was scored by Morton Peto Betts.

West Bromwich Albion. Five time winners of the FA Cup.

3 Cup Fever

In the early years, the FA Cup
was won by amateur clubs.
Wanderers won the FA Cup
five times in the first seven years.
When Spurs first won the Cup in 1901,
they were still a non-league team.

These days, amateur clubs
don't stand much chance of winning the Cup.
But they still try.

In 1994, non-league team Kidderminster
reached the fifth round
before losing 1–0 to West Ham.

The whole world watches the FA Cup final.
But the magic begins nine months earlier,
when hundreds of small clubs
kick off the competition.

These games are not shown on TV.
They don't get big crowds.
But they are part of the magic of the FA Cup.

The small clubs have to play six rounds
before league clubs join in.
Clubs from the premier league
and the first division
don't join until the third round.
It takes a premier league club
five games to reach the final.
It would take some non-league clubs
thirteen games!

4 Giant-killers

Big clubs usually beat the small clubs.
But sometimes it is the other way round.
Anything can happen in the FA Cup.
Everyone likes to see the small clubs
beat the big clubs.
And the bigger they come,
the harder they fall.

Arsenal were once knocked out by Walsall.
Colchester United once beat Leeds.
Manchester United were once
beaten by Bournemouth.
Non-league Yeovil Town
once knocked out Sunderland.

In 1972, non-league Hereford
met Newcastle in the third round.
Hereford were losing 1–0.
Then Ronnie Radford scored
with a 30-yard screamer.
In extra time, Ricky George came on
and scored the winner for Hereford.
Little Hereford were through
to the next round.

In 1973, second division Sunderland
played Leeds in the final.
Leeds were the best team in the country.
But Ian Porterfield scored for Sunderland.
Leeds attacked the Sunderland goal.
But Sunderland keeper Jim Montgomery
played a blinder.
He made a fantastic double save.
Sunderland were cup-winners.

Ron Radford and Rickey George – giant-killers.

The biggest giant-killing took place in 1988
when Wimbledon reached the FA Cup final.
They had only been in the league
for eleven years.
They had never won anything.
And they had to play Liverpool.
Everyone thought Liverpool would win.
But Wimbledon scored.
Then Liverpool were given a penalty.
No one had ever saved a penalty
in the FA Cup Final before.
But Dave Beasant did.
Little Wimbledon had won the FA Cup.

5 The White Horse Final

For the first fifty years,
FA Cup finals were played at lots of grounds.
Since 1923, they have been played
at Wembley.

The 1923 FA Cup final
was between Bolton and West Ham.
Over a quarter of a million people
tried to see the game.
The crowd couldn't fit into the stand.
They spilled out on to the pitch.
The police tried to push the crowd back.
One of the policemen was called George Scorey.
He was riding a white horse called Billy.
Billy helped clear the pitch
so the game could start.
Billy was a hero.

Billy the white horse helps clear the pitch.

There were still too many people.
The crowd were standing on the touchlines
and behind the goal.
After two minutes, the ball went
into the crowd.
A West Ham player went to get the ball back.
The crowd threw the ball on to the pitch.
The game started again and Bolton scored
while the West Ham player was still
trying to get back on the pitch.
Bolton beat West Ham 2–0.

Not many people remember the score that day,
but everyone knows why it was called
the White Horse Final.

6 The Matthews Final

The 1953 FA Cup final
is very famous.
Blackpool versus Bolton.
England winger Stanley Matthews
was playing for Blackpool.
He was thirty-eight.
He was one of the best players
of all time,
but he had never won anything.

Blackpool were 3–1 down
with twenty minutes left.
Then Matthews started dribbling
through the Bolton defence.
He wasn't going to give up.
The crowd went wild.
Matthews ran past a defender,
crossed the ball
and Stan Mortenson scored.
Straight from kick off
Matthews ran through the Bolton defenders again.
A few minutes later the score was 3–3.
In the last seconds,
Matthews beat a defender and raced for goal.
He pulled the ball back across the goal.
4–3!
Thanks to Stanley Matthews,
Blackpool won the cup at last.

Stan Mortenson scored a hat-trick that day,
but everyone calls it the Matthews final.

FA Cup winner Stanley Matthews meets the Queen.

7 Did You Know?

Preston North End once scored
26 goals in an FA Cup game.

Oswestry Town once beat Badsey Rangers 19–3.

Dulwich Hamlet and Wealdstone
once drew an FA Cup game 7–7.

Leicester City have played in
four FA Cup finals,
but they have never won the Cup.

Cardiff City are the only non-English club
to have won the FA Cup.

Leicester City and Middlesbrough
were both relegated
after losing in the FA Cup final.

In 1946, FA Cup ties were played
over two games.

In the 1956 Cup final,
Manchester City keeper Bert Trautmann
was badly injured.
He was hurt but he carried on playing.
He discovered later that he had broken his neck!

Bert Trautmann is helped off the pitch.

Penalty shoot-outs started in 1991.

The first FA Cup final hat-trick
was scored in 1890 by William Towney
for Blackburn Rovers.

The first FA Cup final penalty
was scored by Newcastle United in 1910.

In 1994, Chelsea gave away two penalties
in the FA Cup final.

Bury and Preston North End are the only clubs
who have won the FA Cup
without letting in a single goal.

Chelsea's Peter Osgood
is the only player to score in every round,
including the final.

8 Some FA Cup Stats

Most FA Cup Wins:
Manchester United 10
Arsenal and Spurs 8
Aston Villa 7

Most FA Cup Finals:
Arsenal 15
Manchester United 15
Newcastle United 13

Most FA Cup Semi-Finals:
Everton 23
Arsenal 22
Manchester United 22
Liverpool 21
Aston Villa 19
West Bromwich Albion 19

Biggest FA Cup Final Win:
Bury 6 – Derby County 0

Most FA Cup Goals Scored in a Season:
Aston Villa 40

Most FA Cup Final Goals:
Ian Rush (Liverpool) 5

Most FA Cup Goals:
Henry Cursham (Notts County) 48

Most FA Cup Goals in a Season:
Jimmy Ross (Preston North End) 20

Most Goals in a Single FA Cup Game:
Ted MacDougall (Bournemouth) 9

Youngest Player in an FA Cup Game:
Andy Awford (Worcester City) aged 15

Youngest Player in an FA Cup Final:
James Prinsep (Clapham Rovers) aged 17

Youngest Goal-Scorer in an FA Cup Final:
Norman Whiteside (Manchester United) aged 18

Arsenal celebrate winning the FA Cup in 2002.

9 We're Going to Wembley

In 2003, the famous twin-towers of Wembley
were knocked down.
While it is being re-built,
FA Cup finals are being played
at the Millennium Stadium in Cardiff.
It's an amazing stadium.
It even has a sliding roof to protect the pitch.

Who is going to win the FA Cup this year?
Could it be *your* team?
You never know.
Remember, anything can happen
in the FA Cup.